CUT FLOWER GROWING

Published in 2022 by Hardie Grant Books, an imprint of Hardie Grant Publishing

Hardie Grant Books (London)
5th & 6th Floors
52–54 Southwark Street
London SE1 1UN

Hardie Grant Books (Melbourne)
Building 1, 658 Church Street
Richmond, Victoria 3121

hardiegrantbooks.com

British Library Cataloguing-in-Publication Data. A catalogue record for this book is available from the British Library.

Cut Flower Growing by Marianne Slater

ISBN: 978-1-78488-525-0

10 9 8 7 6 5 4 3 2 1

Publisher: Kajal Mistry
Project Editor: Chelsea Edwards
Design: Claire Warner Studio
Photography: Marianne Slater
Copy Editor: Rosie Fairhead
Proofreader: Jessica Spencer
Indexer: Helen Snaith

Colour Reproduction by p2d
Printed and bound in China
by Leo Paper Products Ltd

*For Alison, without whom,
this book wouldn't exist.*

DISCLAIMER

Every care possible has been taken to give the best advice available on the topics in this book, but the techniques and suggestions all come from my own experience, and tips and tricks I have picked up along the way. I am simply sharing my journey and my experiences with you. Sometimes you can do all the right things and take all the right steps, but your flowers just don't show up. This can be for any number of reasons: weather, soil, poor-quality or old seed, the list goes on – that's nature! Don't be too hard on yourself; keep trying and don't give up.

SAFETY

Please make sure you take all safety precautions necessary and in line with the equipment you choose to use while undertaking any gardening project.

CUT FLOWER GROWING

A BEGINNER'S GUIDE
TO PLANNING, PLANTING
AND STYLING CUT
FLOWERS, WHATEVER
YOUR SPACE

MARIANNE
SLATER

Hardie Grant

BOOKS

INTRODUCTION

Growing cut flowers is, essentially, simple. While it does entail a lot of hard work, for sure, the principles I have used throughout my career have stemmed from adapting straightforward rules to my surroundings and experiences. It is basically a never-ending experiment: year on year you learn what works and what doesn't, and, really, it is applying these lessons throughout your journey that will make you an efficient and successful grower.

WHAT IS A CUT FLOWER?

Cut flowers are what all florists, floral designers and flower arrangers use to create their displays. A cut flower is one that will last well when its stem is cut from the main plant. The flower or foliage is robust enough not to wilt or wither too quickly, and can be enjoyed in arrangements in water for days after cutting.

WHY WOULD YOU WANT TO GROW YOUR OWN CUT FLOWERS?

There are many different reasons. Home-grown cut flowers are much more eco-friendly than most shop-bought ones, some of which have travelled thousands of miles on aircraft, boats or trains to get to your local supermarket or florist. The air miles in even a simple shop-bought bouquet can be astronomically high. I think the most basic reason to grow your own cut flowers, though, is simply to enjoy the process. It is magical to pop seeds into some soil, take care of them, watch them grow and then, when they're ready, cut them, arrange them and enjoy them!

GROWING FLOWERS

IS BASICALLY
A NEVER-ENDING
EXPERIMENT

Chapter 1:

PLANNING & PREPARING

ASSESSING
your aims

Whatever space you have to dedicate to growing cut flowers – whether it is just a few pots, one raised bed or a small field (or more!) – I fully believe that you can grow beautiful flowers to enjoy. Planning is the way to be most efficient with your time and budget. If you know how much space you have to fill and what you want to get out of it, you can make a good plan of how to move forward with dedicating time to your flower garden.

FINDING YOUR INSPIRATION

Take some time over this section and really think about what you want to get out of flower growing. This is the daydream, fantasy part where I suggest you get lost in Pinterest and your own ideas notebook or scrapbook (if you're anything like me, a dedicated 'flower-growing' notebook is a must). My Pinterest boards are where I find so much inspiration, and I find that visualising my goal always helps me to plan.

It's a great idea to look for inspiration that matches the space you have. If you have a small patio in a city, search for something like 'small city garden'. Looking at images of how people have used a meadow-sized garden to start a flower farm can be disheartening when your reality is a much smaller space, but even the smallest space can be beautiful when used properly. Use Pinterest to see how other people have used limited spaces, which pots or containers they have chosen and also how much they have fitted into an area similar to yours. Pinterest vs Reality can be a real demotivator, but if you're searching for the most relevant inspiration for your project it can spark many amazing ideas.

I also keep a notebook on hand or a section in my phone (I have both on the go) for whenever I see something in a garden, on television, in a magazine or on the internet that I might like to try and grow. I either jot it down or print it off/cut it out if it's something really beautiful, then do a little bit of research to see if it's suitable for my garden and whether I can work it into my next growing year.

WHAT AM I HOPING TO GET OUT OF GROWING CUT FLOWERS?

Is it simply the joy of the process and a fresh vase of flowers on the kitchen table every week? A few gift bouquets to share with friends and family? Are you wanting to grow and arrange some flowers for your own wedding or event? Or are you a florist wanting to add variety to your arrangements? Have a think about the scale you want and how that fits the space you have available.

HOW MUCH TIME DO I HAVE FOR THIS PROJECT?

Do you have weekends to yourself, one dedicated day a week, a free evening? It's important to make sure you don't put pressure on yourself to do too much. Flower growing should be an enjoyable (if slightly labour-intensive) journey; it can calm the soul, bring happiness and create true joy. The time you dedicate to it must sit happily within your life, and if you let it become a burden, something you feel chained to, you won't enjoy the fruits of your labour anywhere near as much.

You should come out with enough produce to create pretty arrangements throughout the summer, even if you have only one evening a week to put into this project. If that is the case for you, I would recommend picking a few (between five and ten) varieties of annual seed to grow, and dedicate that time to sowing, nurturing and maintaining them throughout the season.

WHAT SIZE SPACE DO I NEED?

You can grow a surprising amount even in the smallest spaces; a few beds or some pots are all you really need. It is generally agreed that the best size for a flower bed is about 3 by 1 m (10 by 3 ft), so that you can reach all the plants when you're cutting but still fit a few different varieties into each bed. Although this is really sound advice, I would say that, as a rule of thumb, if you can walk around the space comfortably, reach all the plants for cutting and weeding, not hurt yourself at the height you're working at and create a beautiful display of all your favourites, you won't go far wrong. I don't work in raised beds because I have lots of established perennials to work around, and I've never felt that holds me back, but they can be useful if you're working on very poor ground (with a lot of builder's rubble, for example, or on very sandy soil), and they're great if you find it tricky to bend to ground level.

I find my space so much more inspiring for creative arranging if I see my flowers mixed up a little, rather than growing them in tidy rows of single varieties. It's maybe a little unorthodox and not always practical for very large-scale growing, but I don't think there is anything wrong with making the layout of your cut flowers pleasing to the eye (and the soul).

WHAT IF MY SPACE IS VERY SMALL?

If you have only a small balcony or patio, you really can still grow a nice mix of cut flowers to enjoy. Container gardening obviously has its limitations, but if you dedicate your space to some easy 'cut and come again' annuals you should be able to enjoy your produce throughout the summer. Here are my top tips for a very small area:

▶ **Make your space work hard for you.** You can plant bulbs in autumn in pots or containers, enjoy them in spring, lift the bulbs and then reuse the pots to sow annual seed. Then, when these die back in autumn, start the process again.

▶ **Mix things up.** If you want to try perennials, such as astrantia, *Alchemilla* and geum, put them all in one bigger pot (about 50 cm/20 in) together. They will grow to fill the space, and you will be able to enjoy them all together and cut from them evenly.

▶ **Be selective with annual seeds.** I would suggest picking one of my beginner's cut-flower seeds (see page 28) per 30 cm (12 in) pot or space. If you want enough flowers to keep cutting from regularly, plant five to ten seedlings in a space of that size.

► **Start early with annual seeds.**
Sow your seeds in mid spring outside,
or in autumn if you have the space to
keep them inside over winter. This way
you should see flowers earlier in summer
and then have them to enjoy throughout
the year.

► **Grow herbs.** Herbs are amazing for
flower arranging, cooking and drinking.
They are the sort of plant that works hard
for you in a small area, growing profusely
in good conditions and adding amazing
scent and texture to the space. If you have
room for only a few, I would recommend
any type of mint, rosemary and lemon
balm. It can be difficult to find foliage for
flower arrangements, and herbs really are
a lifesaver in that respect.

WHERE TO PLANT?

Ideally, find the spot in your garden that gets the most direct sunlight throughout the day. To thrive, most flowering plants – including all hardy annuals – need around six hours of sun each day, so try to find a space with as little shade as you can and start there. Some plants do better in shade than others, particularly certain perennials, so if you have a mainly shady space, I would recommend looking for shade-tolerant perennials and shrubs like *Alchemilla mollis*, astrantia and suitable roses (individual suppliers are able to recommend the best roses for shade). Unfortunately, if your space is in the shade all day, you will struggle to grow any annual flowers from seed as they need either light, or at least heat which is generated by the sun, in order to germinate.

MATERIALS BUDGET AND LIST

Plants can be expensive, as can tools, and buying all the 'right equipment' can quickly rack up. It is very important to me that growing and enjoying flowers should be accessible to everyone, not just those with a big budget. The advice in this book is aimed at being as resourceful as possible, and while it's ultimately up to you how much you spend, even with just £20–30 ($30–40) to spend on seeds and materials you will be able to grow something! I promise.

You definitely don't need anything fancy to get going with growing flowers, but here's a short list of helpful items:

- *Soil/potting mix/potting compost/ garden compost*
- *Spade*
- *Border fork*
- *Trowel*
- *Hand fork*
- *Pots or containers (see page 37 for creative suggestions for recycling)*
- *Watering can, jug or bottles*
- *Seed markers (see page 38 for creative suggestions for recycling)*
- *Seeds*
- *String*
- *Snips and/or secateurs*
- *Bamboo canes, hazel poles or long metal stakes*
- *Rake*

WHAT TO
grow

It's easy to get bogged down in technical info about the different types of plant. I tend to get the best results from categorising the ones I work with into the five groups listed below and I make sure I have a balance of them on my plot. The bulk of what I grow (about 80 per cent) is hardy annuals, biennials, bulbs, tubers, corms and roses; these are topped up with perennials and foliage plants such as shrubs and climbers.

ANNUALS

These are plants that germinate, grow, flower and die within a single year. They come from seeds sown either in autumn or in spring, bloom in late spring and give flowers throughout the summer into autumn, until the frost comes. Once they die, they go to seed, which means the plant turns its energy from the production of flowers to the production of seeds.

Clockwise from top left: cosmos, foxglove, phlox.

These seeds can be harvested for sowing next year, to maintain your stock. I mainly grow hardy annuals, because they do better in the cool weather we get here in the UK. These are a cut-flower-grower's bread and butter, and what I will concentrate on in this book. Examples are *Ammi*, *Nigella* and sweet peas. Half-hardy annuals, like phlox and cosmos are also great for cut flowers, but they don't like the wet and cold of the winter so must be started off and grown under cover before they are planted out after the last frost. They will not last as late into the season as the hardy annuals should, dying off as soon as it gets too cold.

BIENNIALS

Plants that don't flower in their first year but do in their second. These are really useful when planted during summer, when they will develop a leafy mass that lasts through winter and then gives you flowers next spring, helping to fill any gaps from annuals yet to bloom. Examples are foxgloves, sweet William, honesty, wallflowers.

Clockwise
from top left:
tulips, cherry
blossom, dahlia.

BULBS, TUBERS, CORMS AND RHIZOMES

DIE BACK
AND REGROW
EACH YEAR

BULBS, TUBERS, CORMS AND RHIZOMES

These plants grow from underground storage organs, flower, then die back before regrowing the following year. Normally planted in winter or early spring, depending on the type, they add great interest and gorgeous colour to the garden and to arrangements, and I wouldn't be without them. Some you can reuse year after year, but others are more successful if they are planted anew each year. There is more on my favourite varieties on page 53 (Beyond annuals). Examples are tulips, dahlias, ranunculus.

CLIMBERS, SHRUBS AND TREES

These types are all perennial in nature, since they come back each year, but all have slightly different seasonal patterns of growth. Depending on the variety, you can make up a fuller year of flowers and foliage with tree blossoms and shrubs because many of them produce material for flower arranging during the colder months. Climbers are wonderful for adding coverage to outside structures. Because of their twining, curling habit, their stems are very interesting for arranging, and they are usually vigorous growers, needing little care. Examples are lilac and holly (trees), *Viburnum* and Japanese quince (shrubs), honeysuckle and clematis (climbers).

PERENNIALS

Perennials – any plant that lasts for three
years or more – generally die back
in the colder months and regrow their
foliage in spring, flowering in summer
and autumn depending on the variety.
Examples are peonies, *Rudbeckia* and lupins.

OTHER GROWING CONSIDERATIONS

Pollinators

By choosing to grow your own flowers, you are already connecting with nature in an amazing way. By adding a few flowers that are great for pollinators you're encouraging biodiversity as well as helping the ecosystem in your area to thrive. It's also lovely to watch bees, butterflies and other insects enjoying your flowers and your space.

Scent

Not all flowers for cutting will have a vast amount of scent, and some may have none at all. That's why, if you are looking to bring the smells of the garden into your home, you should choose a few varieties that are highly scented. My favourites for scent are always sweet peas, which are very easy to grow in a pot. I would also highly recommend adding herbs to your growing selection if possible. I wouldn't be without mint or lemon balm, and also lavender, which is an amazingly special scent to add to arrangements and is also brilliant for drying.

Opposite: peony.
Above: cosmos.
Below: sweet pea.

MY
favourites

These are the flowers and foliage that I use most in my arrangements. I have listed them by season (meaning the season in which they flower and can be used), and for annuals, biennials and bulbs I also give details of when to plant them.

While this list does not give *everything* I have ever used in my work or grown on my plot, it is a pretty comprehensive collection of the flowers I enjoy throughout the year.

WHERE TO GET YOUR SEEDS AND PLANTS?

I get my seeds and plants from various places, including online stores, nurseries, RHS (Royal Horticultural Society in the UK) shows, garden suppliers, other grower friends and colleagues and open gardens. I have suggested my favourite online places to buy seeds and plants in the Resources section on page 142.

I like to find places that grow and nurture their plants near me. These local nurseries and garden suppliers are a great place to discover new varieties and find out what they grow, as these will generally be good in my garden as well. This also works for local open gardens, where gardeners might split their plants to sell, harvest their own seeds for you to buy or just have interesting planting variations to inspire you.

I also find flower shows and the gardens of public attractions are great for inspiration. Often they will have spaces dedicated to cut flowers and cut-flower growing, great for new ideas, inspiration and purchasing.

I keep good company with my other flowergrowing friends and colleagues (they are always the best people). So if you know anyone else who is growing things at the same time as you, you could always set up a seed or seedling swap, ask for recommendations, and generally support each other during the process.

WINTER AND EARLY SPRING

NAME	TYPE	NOTES	
Anemone (*Anemone*)	corm	planted in winter or early spring	
Daffodil (*Narcissus*)	bulb	planted in early winter	
Grape hyacinth (*Muscari armeniacum*)	bulb	planted in early winter	
Hellebore (*Helleborus*)	perennial		
Holly (*Ilex*)	shrub		
Hyacinth (*Hyacinthus*)	bulb	planted in early winter	
Ivy (*Hedera helix*)	woody climber	great berries	
Japanese quince (*Chaenomeles japonica*)	shrub		
Pussy willow (*Salix caprea*)	shrub/tree		
Ranunculus (*Ranunculus*)	corm	planted in winter or early spring	
Sage (*Salvia*)	shrub		
Spruce (*Picea*)	shrub/tree		
Tulip (*Tulipa*)	bulb	planted in early winter	
Various blossoms such as fruit-producing trees such as quince, apple and cherry	shrub/tree		

🌸 great for scent   🐝 great for pollinators

SPRING

NAME	TYPE	NOTES	
Corncockle (*Agrostemma githago*)	annual		
Cornflower (*Centaurea cyanus*)	seed	autumn- or spring-sown annual	
Euphorbia (*Euphorbia*)	perennial		
Foxglove (*Digitalis*)	seed	early summer-sown biennial	🐝
Geum (*Geum*)	perennial		🐝
Granny's bonnet (*Aquilegia*)	perennial		🐝
Honesty (*Lunaria annua*)	seed	autumn- or spring-sown annual/biennial	
Lilac (*Syringa*)	shrub		❀ 🐝
Mint (*Mentha*)	perennial herb		❀
Ornamental onion (*Allium*)	bulb	planted in early winter	🐝
Pansy and violet (*Viola*)	seed	perennial	🐝
Peony (*Paeonia*)	perennial	subtle scent	❀
Poppy (*Papaver*)	perennial		🐝
Solomon's seal (*Polygonatum × hybridum*)	perennial		🐝
Sweet pea (*Lathyrus odoratus*)	seed	autumn- or spring-sown annual	❀
Sweet William (*Dianthus barbatus*)	seed	early summer-sown biennial	❀ 🐝
Tulip (*Tulipa*)	bulb	planted in early winter	
Wallflower (*Erysimum*)	seed	autumn- or spring-sown biennial	❀ 🐝

❀ great for scent   🐝 great for pollinators

LATE SPRING AND EARLY SUMMER

NAME	TYPE	NOTES	
Annual scabious (*Scabiosa*)	seed	autumn- or spring-sown annual	🐝
Astrantia (*Astrantia*)	perennial		🐝
Bellflower (*Campanula*)	perennial		🐝
Bishop's flower (*Ammi majus*)	seed	autumn- or spring-sown annual	
Clary sage (*Salvia sclarea*)	seed	autumn- or spring-sown annual	
Feverfew (*Tanacetum parthenium*)	perennial		
Foxglove (*Digitalis*)	seed	autumn- or spring-sown biennial	🐝
Honesty (*Lunaria annua*)	seed	late spring-sown biennial great seed heads	
Lady's mantle (*Alchemilla mollis*)	perennial		
Love-in-a-mist (*Nigella damascena*)	seed	autumn- or spring-sown annual	🐝
Love-lies-bleeding (*Amaranthus*)	seed	autumn- or spring-sown annual	
Poppy seed heads (*Papaver*)	seed	spring-sown annual	
Queen Anne's lace (*Daucus carota*)	seed	autumn- or spring-sown annual	
Rose (*Rosa*) – many varieties	shrub		❀
Rosemary (*Salvia rosmarinus*)	shrubby herb		❀
Sea holly (*Eryngium*)	both annual and perennial varieties		
Scabious (*Knautia macedonica*)	perennial		🐝
Yarrow (*Achillea*)	perennial		🐝

❀ great for scent   🐝 great for pollinators

SUMMER

NAME	TYPE	NOTES	
Clematis (*Clematis*)	perennial climber		🐝
Cosmos (*Cosmos*)	seed	autumn- or spring-sown annual	🐝
Dahlia (*Dahlia*)	tuber	planted in spring	
Dill (*Anethum graveolens*)	seed	autumn- or spring-sown annual	🐝
Fennel (*Foeniculum vulgare*)			
Honeysuckle (*Lonicera*)	perennial climber		🌼 🐝
Jasmine (*Jasminum*)	perennial climber		🌼
Larkspur (*Consolida ajacis*)	seed	autumn- or spring-sown annual	🐝
Lavender (*Lavandula*)	perennial		🌼 🐝
Love-in-a-mist (*Nigella damascena*)	seed	autumn- or spring-sown annual great seed heads	
Marigold (*Calendula*)	seed	autumn- or spring-sown annual	🐝
Phlox (*Phlox*)	seed	autumn- or spring-sown annual	🐝
Rose (*Rosa*) – many varieties	shrub		🌼
Scabious (*Scabiosa*)	seed	autumn- or spring-sown annual	🐝
Sedum (*Sedum/Hylotelephium*)	perennial		🐝
Snapdragon (*Antirrhinum*)	seed	autumn- or spring-sown annual	
Sweet pea (*Lathyrus odoratus*)	seed	autumn- or spring-sown annual	🌼
Verbena (*Verbena*)	seed	autumn- or spring-sown annual	🐝
Veronica (*Veronica*)	perennial		🐝

🌼 great for scent   🐝 great for pollinators

AUTUMN

NAME	TYPE	NOTES	
Annual sage (*Salvia*)	seed	autumn- or spring-sown annual	🐝
Black-eyed Susan (*Rudbeckia*)	annual or perennial, depending on variety		
Chrysanthemum (*Chrysanthemum*)	perennial		🐝
Coneflower (*Echinacea*)	perennial		🐝
Cosmos (*Cosmos*)	seed	autumn- or spring-sown annual	
Dahlia (*Dahlia*)	tuber	planted in spring	✿
Dill (*Anethum graveolens*)	seed	autumn- or spring-sown annual	🐝
Helenium (*Helenium*)	annual or perennial, depending on variety		🐝
Marigold (*Calendula*)	seed	autumn- or spring-sown annual	
Michaelmas daisy (*Aster*)	perennial		✿
Phlox (*Phlox*)	seed	autumn- or spring-sown annual	✿
Rose (*Rosa*) – many varieties	shrub		✿
Rosemary (*Salvia rosmarinus*)	shrubby herb		✿
Scabious (*Scabiosa*)	seed	autumn- or spring-sown annual	🐝
Sedum (*Sedum/Hylotelephium*)	perennial		
Sunflower (*Helianthus*)	seed	autumn- or spring-sown annual	✿
Sweet pea (*Lathyrus odoratus*)	seed	autumn- or spring-sown annual	
Various grasses (*Panicum elegans, Panicum miliaceum, Briza maxima, Lagurus*)	some annual, some perennial		
Various seed heads (*Poppy, nigella, ammi*)	seed	autumn- or spring-sown annuals	

✿ great for scent   🐝 great for pollinators

This may seem like a gigantic list, so I suggest you find a few favourites among the different varieties and seasons and just have a go. A packet of seeds can go a long way and you will be able to use any leftovers next year as well, so if you do order too many (as I usually do), don't panic – they will all have their moment.

SUGGESTIONS *for beginners*

Here are some suggestions for beginners who want to try out sowing annual and biennial seeds. All will give great material for flower arranging:

Bishop's flower (*Ammi majus*)

Clary sage (*Salvia sclarea*)

Cornflower (*Centaurea cyanus*)

Cosmos (*Cosmos*)

Dill (*Anethum graveolens*)

Fennel (*Foeniculum vulgare*)

Foxgloves (*Digitalis*)

Granny's bonnet (*Aquilegia*)

Grasses (*Briza, Lagurus, Pennisetum,* etc.)

Honesty (*Lunaria annua;* for seed heads)

Larkspur (*Consolida ajacis*)

Love-in-a-mist (*Nigella damascena;* for flowers and seed heads)

Love-lies-bleeding (*Amaranthus*)

Phlox (*Phlox*)

Poppy (*Papaver;* for flowers and seed heads)

Queen Anne's lace (*Daucus carota*)

Scabious (*Knautia macedonica*)

Snapdragon (*Antirrhinum*)

Sunflower (*Helianthus*)

Sweet pea (*Lathyrus odoratus*)

Verbena (*Verbena*)

White laceflower (*Orlaya grandiflora*)

Yarrow (*Achillea*)

FROM SEED TO

CUTTING

GETTING STARTED
with growing

In this section we will take a comprehensive look at the process of starting a cutting garden.

We will concentrate on growing from seed at first, and then cover other plants such as roses, dahlias and those that come from bulbs and corms.

You will need to start off your autumn- and spring-sown seedlings inside. Whether that is on windowsills in your home, or in a greenhouse or potting shed, just make sure it's somewhere with good natural light.

SEED TRAYS

You'll need trays or pots to start your seeds off in. Don't worry too much about buying dedicated plant pots – you can be creative and reuse containers such as plastic or Tetra Pak cartons, tin cans or yoghurt pots. Basically, anything that is waterproof and around 10–15 cm (4–6 in) deep will be just fine, as long as it's clean. They should have small holes in the bottom for drainage, which you can make (carefully!) with sharp snips or a nail. You will also need to put these pots and trays into or on to something waterproof *without* holes to catch the water in, otherwise you'll make a giant mess!

POTS, PLANTERS AND CONTAINERS

As with the seed trays and pots, any larger pots, planters or containers, including those you are using as a final destination for your cut flowers, must be clean and have drainage holes. If you are using really big pots as your final planters, these will need a good layer of rubble underneath the compost (depending on the size of your container, fill up to 5–10 per cent of the overall depth), such as broken ceramics, pebbles or rocks to aid drainage. If you're using planters for your final cutting garden, make sure they have adequate drainage, a layer of rubble and a good-quality potting medium. A good peat-free, all-purpose compost from the garden centre will be fine. You can mix in some fertiliser when you plant things out, if it's available, but this is not essential. Avoid basic topsoil if possible as it is can contain field soil which might be full of weeds, sand and other low-nutrient additions.

FLOWER BEDS

If you're using flower beds, as I said in the planning stage, these should be created with your space in mind, making sure you have adequate room for paths, planting and weeding. Edging them with planks will ensure they look neat and will define the paths between them, resulting in an ordered space. But don't worry if you don't have the equipment for this; just be sure to edge your beds neatly with a sharp spade, which will help to keep weeds and grass under control and out of your growing space.

To prepare the beds for your plants, you need to turn the soil so it's disturbed and becomes loose and aerated rather than being solid and clumpy. You can start digging it over with a spade, then use a border fork to break it up further. I would also go over it with a rake, if possible, before you start planting, to break up any last lumps and give you nice fine soil – what gardeners and farmers call a 'fine tilth'.

RAISED BEDS

Raised beds are great for gardens with poor soil as the boxed container allows you to add better soil on top. You want the raised bed to be at least 30–45 cm deep (12–18 in). You should fill it with a mix of 40 per cent compost, 40 per cent bagged topsoil and 20 per cent drainage at the bottom, because even if the bed goes into soil, you still need to make sure the soil drains well.

GREENHOUSES AND COVERINGS

I know it's not possible or practical for everyone to have a greenhouse, but making space for some sort of covered growing structure can be very useful when growing cut flowers. By creating cover for your plants, you can extend their growing time over periods when the weather would be too cold for them to grow unprotected. You can sow seeds earlier, meaning they will produce flowers sooner, and you can keep some of your produce growing later in the season. For example, I put an inexpensive plastic 'greenhouse tent' over my dahlias when I'm worried about frost in autumn.

If you don't have the space or budget for a greenhouse, there are several ways of covering seedlings. Prop up old, empty picture frames to create a cover, or make a DIY cold frame using old window frames. Clear-plastic storage boxes work well, up-turned over the plants.

Of course, make sure you weigh all these down so they don't take off in the wind. Smaller options are clear plastic food trays, ziplock bags or simply a loose layer of clingfilm over seed trays (just make sure it never touches the emerging seedlings, or you'll have problems with mould and fungus). Whatever you choose, make sure you check on all covered plants every day and water if necessary to make sure they don't dry out.

TIP:
*Horse manure
is an amazing
fertiliser to enrich
your soil.*

I get mine from a neighbour
and collect it in old compost bags.
One bag of manure is usually
enough for two of my raised beds,
and I rake it through the top of the
soil once a year, just before I plant
my seedlings into the ground.

A NOTE ON DIRECT SOWING

If you don't have lots of space indoors for trays of seedlings, you can wait until later in the spring (once all fear of frost has passed) and sow your seeds directly into their final pots, beds or containers. You have less control with this method – you can end up with lots of plants in one area, or none, because they're more vulnerable to pests outside – but it's a really good, basic way to get some things going if you're short of space. The seeds I mentioned on page 28 as the best for beginners are all ones I would happily sow directly.

STARTING
your seeds

SOWING

First things first, a piece of advice from my dad: 'If you can read, you can cook.' If we apply this to seed packets, you're already halfway to a thriving collection of seed-grown flowers.

Different seeds will need different environments to germinate, so once you've chosen and bought them, I find it helpful to start by laying the seed packets out on a large table in piles based on the month they say they should be sown. Then, sub-group these piles according to the temperature at which the packet says germination occurs. I find a folder or a box with tabs and plastic pockets very useful for organising my seed packets – it helps to simplify things.

Working in small batches, sow the seeds according to the instructions on the packet (some need to go on top of the soil, some into the soil to a specific depth). I try to recycle as many single-use plastic containers and tins as possible for this, as well as plastic and paper plant pots. Just make sure any reused containers are cleaned with a little bleach and water first.

Always use peat-free compost specifically for seedlings; you can always pot on into your own compost later, once the seedlings are well grown. Sow into moist soil, making sure not to overwater them – using a sprayer to water works really well with delicate new seedlings. If they need more warmth for germination than your room or greenhouse provides, you can cover them with clingfilm or glass. Just make sure the covering doesn't touch the new seedlings as they come up.

RECORD-KEEPING

Try to make sure you date and label everything you sow. I am notorious for forgetting to label things, and while it isn't the end of the world, it's pretty annoying, especially if you want to end up with a nice, neat bed, pot or row of one single thing.

I have tried out many different labelling methods over the years: white plastic with black marker pen; chalkboards and chalk markers; wooden lollipop sticks and biro; reused strips of plastic tubs and Sharpie – basically everything you can think of. All have their problems: some, the writing wears off, some rot, lots just go missing. I think permanent marker on a white plastic tag is the clearest and most simple method, and these can be made easily by cutting up washed yoghurt pots and similar tubs. Try to collect them up and store them so that you can clean and reuse them if you grow the same things each year.

If you are planning to grow a lot, you will find it very useful to make a chart in your notebook to show when you sowed something and when you planted it out. This helps you to understand the timelines and is also great to look back at when you start again next year.

ASSESSING WHAT'S GROWN

An essential part of the growing process is to pay attention to what's growing well, what needs more space and assessing what might need moving on. Once your seedlings have germinated, they will need space to establish a strong root system. It's important to thin out your seedlings as soon as they are ready, which is usually when the first true leaves emerge (usually the second set). There will be differences with all varieties of seedlings, so pay attention to the packet instructions when deciding when to separate your seedlings.

Prepare deeper trays or pots full of moist compost and then select the strongest of your seedlings. Using a dibber or pencil, make a hole in the soil in the new container and then, one by one, gently extract the selected seedlings, keeping the root intact. Put them in the hole you've made and make sure they are firmly in place by pressing down the surrounding soil.

POTTING ON

Many seedlings will benefit from an 'in-between' stage before they are hardened off and planted up in their final bed, planter or large pot. This applies to seeds that have been sown in small trays or pots, and it will give the seedlings room to develop stronger, larger roots and stop them from becoming pot-bound (with a root system that is crammed into the pot) while allowing them to spend longer in pots before they go outside. This isn't necessary if you have sown your seeds later in the season, and of course it doesn't apply to seedlings sown directly outside. Seeds that are sown later can go out at a younger stage and establish their roots in the outside soil.

Get clean, larger pots ready for your seedlings, filled with a mix of peat-free compost and your own compost if you like, and transfer the plants. Keep them upright and supported and give them plenty of water. If the root system has become a little pot-bound (you can tell because it will appear matted), massage the roots gently with your fingers to loosen them before transferring the seedling; just be careful not to crush the delicate fibres.

Clockwise
from top:
sowing seeds,
cosmos seedlings
and ranunculus
sprouting.

CHAPTER 2: FROM SEED TO CUTTING

HARDENING OFF

To get used to the outside environment, your seedlings will need to gradually increase the time they spend outdoors. Start with two or three hours each day, in the middle of the day, and increase the duration every few days. If there is no threat of frost, after about a week of putting them in and out, you can leave them outside for a further week or two until they are happy outside plants and are ready to be planted out. Keep an eye on the weather, though; a frost can ruin weeks of work, so make sure you don't leave them out overnight if one is forecast. This is when a cold frame really comes into its own, because you can lift off the cover and replace it really easily, saving you the hassle of having to move pots around all the time.

PLANTING OUT

This is a lot like the potting-on process, except that the final destination is your prepared bed, planter or large pot/container.

Have a full watering can and a bag or bucket of compost by your side. Prepare large pots or planters with your drainage material, (fill up to 5–10 per cent of the overall depth of your container with broken ceramics, pebbles or rocks to aid drainage, underneath the compost) and make sure flower beds are free of weeds. Dig a hole slightly larger than the pot the plant is in, then remove the plant gently from its pot and squeeze the roots

to encourage them to make new roads into their next home. Fill the hole with water, then, as it drains away, place the plant in the hole, filling in around it with compost and pressing the root ball in firmly. If you have your own compost, it's a good idea to sprinkle some around the new plants. Then give everything a generous watering. Leave enough space between the plants for them to grow and thrive: about 20–30 cm (8–12 in) should do.

PINCHING OUT

This type of pruning is perfect for branching annual plants, those that produce several stems and lots of flowers, and should not be used on varieties that produce just a single stem per plant such as sunflowers and zinnias. It encourages branching plants to grow in fullness and bushiness rather than going straight up and becoming too tall – what is sometimes called 'leggy'.

Pinching out should be done to healthy young plants that are about 20–30 cm (8–12 in) tall. Use sharp snips and cut immediately above a set of leaves, about 10 cm (4 in) from the top of the plant. It feels brutal, but it's just science. Doing this signals to the plant to send out more side shoots, meaning more branches and therefore more flowers on nice long stems.

CARING
for your plants

SUPPORT

Once your seedlings are happily
shooting up, the next stage in ensuring
your flowers are protected from strong
winds is to support them, which is also
known as staking. Just about all hardy
annuals mentioned in this book will need
some form of support to keep them from
falling over and allow them to grow tall.
If in doubt, stake – it's easier to do when
the plant is small than when it is too large
and already flopping all over the place.
You can always remove a support if it
becomes clear that it's not going to be
needed by this particular plant.

There are a few ways to stake. I buy pea
netting and support it at the corners
with bamboo canes, making sure to leave
space so that I can get my hands in to cut
stems and tackle weeds. You can make
a similar net by criss-crossing string or
twine between bamboo canes. Bamboo
canes or hazel sticks can be fashioned
into a wigwam shape and tied together
with twine. You can also buy proprietary
metal structures from garden suppliers,
although this is the more expensive option.

Whatever you choose, leave large enough
gaps that the stems can keep growing, but
small enough to stop them from flopping
over. As your plants get taller you may need
to add another layer of netting further up,
and you may also need to tie the stems to
your netting or frame to keep them in place.

> **MAKE A HOLE IN OLD
> WINE CORKS AND PUSH
> THEM ONTO THE TOP ENDS
> OF YOUR BAMBOO CANES**
>
> TO STOP YOU POKING
> YOUR EYE OUT WHEN
> YOU BEND OVER YOUR
> FLOWER BEDS

DEADHEADING

You should now have flowers growing
and coming into bloom. The next stage
is the best bit – enjoying your bounty!
But the work isn't quite over yet as, with
most annuals, the best way to keep them

Clockwise from top left: cosmos seedlings, supported dahlias and sweet peas growing on a bamboo structure.

CHAPTER 2: FROM SEED TO CUTTING

going is to cut them. You may have heard the phrase 'cut and come again', and this is exactly what you must do. Cut off the dead and dying flowers before they go to seed, in order to get more flowers. When a flower goes to seed it signals to the plant that it's time to put all its energy into making that seed, rather than more flowers, and we don't want that. Cut just above a leaf or side shoot.

Allowing your flowers to go to seed is a choice and when you are ready you can also use these as decorative seed heads. With things like honesty, *Nigella* and poppies, we often grow an amount of these specifically just for their seed heads. They look great both dried and fresh and add great interest to arrangements.

WEEDING

A weed is any plant that you don't want in that particular place. Keep weeds under control so that the plants you've chosen to grow have full use of the space you've dedicated to them. If they have to share space – not to mention water, light and nutrients – with other, unwanted plants, this will impact their growth and flower-producing ability.

It's best to remove weeds right down to and including their roots. It can seem easier and quicker just to remove their leaves above the soil, but that won't stop them from coming back. Some – such as dandelions – have a single long root that you will need to dig out with a trowel or hand fork.

I would recommend not using any form of chemical weedkiller, since even those that claim to be environmentally friendly aren't. They all contain chemicals and I just don't see them as compatible with growing flowers or trying to encourage insects and wildlife into the garden.

One of the best ways to prevent weeds is to smother them with matting or a weed-suppressing membrane. You may have seen flower farmers use this and grow their flowers only through holes in the matting. While that is arguably the best way to grow huge numbers of plants, it's not always practical for the smaller garden where space is at a premium. However, if you are able to use matting for the paths between your beds, you'll save yourself from weeding the paths as well. You can always cover it with wood chippings for a more pleasing look.

If you're not sure whether an unidentified plant is a weed or something you're intending to grow, try an identifying app such as PlantNet or LeafSnap. You might even want to keep a weed if you find it pretty. Just because it might traditionally be seen as a 'weed', doesn't mean it can't be appreciated in your space. I use self-seeded wild foxgloves, a variety of glorious grasses and cow parsley, among other things, in my arrangements, despite the fact that those are definitely classed as weeds by some people.

HARVESTING

When harvesting your flowers, be sure to do so at a time of day when the sun isn't beating down. Early morning and dusk are the best times – better for the flowers and their longevity, and much better for the humans doing the picking, too.

Make sure you have a sharp pair of snips and a clean bucket of fresh, cold water with you. Flowers that are already at their fullest will not live for long in the vase, so choose blooms that are not yet fully open. Everything you cut must go straight into the bucket of water. There will be time for stripping leaves and trimming stems later, but the most important thing right now is that they're in water as soon as possible.

CONDITIONING

Conditioning is the key to getting the best vase life out of your flowers, and it essentially means giving them time to drink lots of water before you arrange them. It's very important to disinfect any container you're putting flowers into, so make sure your bucket is clean and then fill it with fresh, cold water. Strip the bottom third of each stem of its leaves and offshoots, then, using sharp snips, cut a few centimetres (an inch or so) at the bottom of the stems at an angle (keep them long for now and cut to correct length when arranging). Stand them in the cold water, away from excessive heat and light, overnight if possible. Then you are ready to start arranging.

ECO
growing

Whenever I can, I keep my growing practices as eco-friendly as possible. After all, we want to work with nature, not against it, when we're growing flowers. Here are my top suggestions for caring for the environment as you work with flowers:

▸ Use biodegradable string or natural twine instead of plastic string or cable ties when you are staking your plants and tying them to support structures. If you do use plastic netting, collect it up carefully at the end of the year and reuse it.

▸ Reuse plastic pots as much as possible. Keep them clean and try not to break them when potting on.

▸ Use plastic food packaging as seed trays or covers for seedlings, rather than buying new, purpose-made pots and trays.

▸ Make your own seedling pots out of newspaper, toilet-roll tubes or yoghurt pots.

▸ Buy peat-free compost. Peat has long been used to enrich commercially sold compost products, but in recent years the damage caused by using and mining peat

has become more and more apparent. Peat is formed through the decomposition of bog plants and, like coal, it is a finite resource; in addition, the mining process destroys unique areas of biodiversity. When peat is mined and spread in the garden, it begins to emit carbon dioxide and methane, all adding to the greenhouse gases in the atmosphere.

▸ Compost your organic waste if possible.

▸ Get your hands on local manure. Places to try are farms (even urban farms) and stables.

▸ Grow flowers that are beloved by pollinators – chiefly bees and other insects – such as foxgloves, scabious, cosmos and *Calendula* (you'll find more in the lists on pages 23–27).

▸ Avoid chemical pesticides. These are a huge no-no for supporting wildlife in your cutting garden, and are incredibly damaging to the ecosystem. A healthy, biodiverse garden is the best natural pest control you can get; adding plants such as *Calendula*, mint and thyme will encourage beneficial bugs to your garden and attracting birds, frogs and newts will help control slugs, snails and caterpillars. So, installing a bird box or mini pond could do wonders for the pest control situation in your garden.

▸ In addition to encouraging wildlife with a penchant for slugs, make sure you use natural slug repellents rather than chemical ones. These can be things such as beer traps (beer in a shallow tray sunk into the soil so that the top is level with the top of the soil), barriers (crushed eggshells or seashells around the base of plants) and proprietary organic slug repellent (those that don't contain metaldehyde).

▸ Collect rainwater in a water butt and use it to water your plants. You should still use fresh, clean water for seedlings as much as possible to avoid spreading infection to these vulnerable plants, but when it comes to shrubs, perennials and strongly growing annuals, rainwater is great. If you have a greenhouse or shed, it's a good idea to add guttering to collect even more.

COMPOSTING

If you have space for compost bins, I would highly recommend them. You can get rid of a lot of household waste this way, including vegetable peelings and eggshells, and of course the green waste from your garden itself. As well as being an eco-friendly,

satisfying and low-cost way of disposing of organic waste and obtaining buckets of lovely growing medium, it can be the perfect home for toads – the anti-slug champion. Finally, if you create a built structure for composting, it can act as a great windbreak in exposed or gusty areas.

If you have room, two or even three compost bins are optimal. In the first bin, you can layer grass cuttings, kitchen and garden waste, cardboard and newspaper, and then, once this bin is full, turn the contents and, if your bin doesn't have a lid, lay something over the top to keep it as warm as possible. Old carpet or cardboard are ideal for this job.

Then you can move on to filling the second bin while the contents of the first break down. By the time the second bin is full, the contents of the first should be ready to use. Then you can turn the contents of the second bin, cover it and, if you have a third bin, make a start on filling that. With the luxury of three bins you will end up with one full of rotted compost that you can use, one that is filling up with organic matter and one that is breaking down. A magnificent system!

If you have no space for any type of composting system, there is nothing wrong with relying on shop-bought compost. It's also a good idea to contact your local authority to see what they do with the garden waste they collect. Many supply that compost to the general public, so it's always worth checking what's available.

Above: crushed
eggshells protect
plant from pests.
Below: double
compost bin.

CHAPTER 2: FROM SEED TO CUTTING

BEYOND
annuals

BULBS

There are many different bulbs you might choose to add to your annuals. My spring garden wouldn't be the same without them, and, as one of the first signs of the season, they are a delightful marker in the growing year. They are also great for growing in pots or containers, so brilliant for smaller spaces. I mainly grow tulips and *Narcissi*, a few *Alliums* and some *Camassia*. Plant these in winter, ideally before the first frost when the ground really starts to harden, so that they can begin to form roots before that happens.

Tips on planting bulbs:

- In a bed or in the ground, dig a hole twice as deep as the height of the bulb. Make sure you put the bulb in the right way up, so that the roots are pointing down and the tip up. Cover with soil, and water well.

- If planting in pots (at least 30 cm deep/ 12 in), you can put two layers of bulbs one on top of the other. Make sure you fill the pot at least halfway with soil before you begin planting, then add the first layer of bulbs, spacing them out so that they're not touching. Cover them with soil, then add a layer of soil equivalent to the depth of a bulb, then a second layer of bulbs and another layer of soil on top. Mixing tulips, crocuses, hyacinths and daffodils in each layer will give you some lovely flowers throughout spring.

It is perfectly possible to use bulbs more than once, although most will produce smaller blooms in subsequent years. There are a couple of ways of doing this. You can lift them, a process in which you cut off the flowers but not the leaves, allowing those to die back into the ground so that the bulb can store nutrients for next year. Once the leaves have died back completely, you can dig the bulbs up, store them in a cool, dry place (don't forget to label them) and plant them again in the autumn. Keep out of reach of pets and children as many bulbs are poisonous.

Alternatively, you can leave them in the ground and they should come back next year. Some varieties are more successful than others in this respect; tulips are notoriously unreliable, but naturalised crocuses and daffodils can come back for decades and actually increase in number over the years. Again, you must cut off the flowers and let the leaves die back into the soil, but remember where they are as you must be careful not to disturb the dormant bulbs with any deep digging. You could use this space for direct sowing some annual seeds, which shouldn't disturb the bulbs too much.

I tend to leave my bulbs in the ground and also buy new ones annually. That gives me a good mix and back-ups if I need them – plus I get to try new varieties each year!

CORMS

Corms, such as ranunculus and anemones, need activating before you plant them. Start this process in midwinter by laying them on a tray of soil in the greenhouse or a warm room. Keep them moist and wait until they sprout green shoots, which shows they are ready to be potted up. The next stages are the same as with potting on and hardening off seedlings (see page 41).

I lift my corms each year straight after they have flowered and died back, remove the soil, dry them off and store them in a cool, dry place for next year, when I will need to start the activation process again in mid winter.

PERENNIALS

I am incredibly lucky to have a number of established perennials in my garden. Things like astrantia, scabious and

geums really are invaluable as cut flowers. Perennials can all be rather challenging to grow from seed, and the success rate can be quite bleak, so – while I don't want to discourage you from trying – it is much easier to buy them as established plants or plug plants. This can be slightly more expensive than growing from seed, but when you weigh up the time spent on attempting to grow them from seed, it can be more cost-effective just to plant healthy plants from a nursery or garden supplier.

The other benefit of some perennials like these is that you can split many of them once they are established. That means you can create two or three plants from one single one, and produce even more flowers. Things this works well with are astrantia, sedum and *Eryngium*.

TUBERS

Dahlias are my all-time favourite flower! These alien-looking tubers are such a wonder that I end up growing huge numbers of the things just because I can't say no. There is a wealth of technical information available elsewhere on splitting dahlias and taking cuttings, but for now let's keep things simple.

In early spring, take the root mass that you have (either purchased new or from the previous year) and plant it in a large or medium-sized pot (approximately 60 cm deep, 60 cm – 2 ft – wide or larger) in a mixture of new compost and your own (if you have it).

Clockwise
from top:
ranunculus,
dahlia and
sedum.

CHAPTER 2: FROM SEED TO CUTTING

You want the tuber to be around 10 cm (4 in)under the soil. Once potted up, keep them inside until they begin to sprout and produce lots of leaves. They don't particularly need lots of light at this stage, but they don't want to get too cold, and you must keep them safe from any chance of frost.

The hardening-off process is important for dahlias. They must acclimatise to being outside before they are planted out, which should be in early summer unless you live in an area that is prone to extremely late frosts. By mid summer you should see the first flowers coming to life, and then you can jump for joy!

Once the flowers are over, when the frost has come, I lift the tubers, knock off all the soil, dry them and store them for next year. If you live in a milder climate they may last left in the ground, but there is still a risk that they will rot and not come back up. I use crates lined with newspaper to keep them from rotting.

Peonies are one of the big hitters with traditional florists and something I get asked for, and about, a lot. I have a few varieties in my borders and, as they are perennial, my peony husbandry is fairly simple. They have a small window of flowering, which is late spring into summer, and they need full sun and plenty of space to be floriferous. As for the plant care, mulch in spring and cut back the old stems in autumn. Be aware that they can take

a few years to get established and give you any flowers, so don't give up on them if they aren't flourishing immediately. Patience and optimism are key! In terms of harvesting and usage, they are one of the trickier cut flowers to deal with, they come into bud as a tight ball and this then develops into a petal ball which will eventually open out into the magnificent flower that is a peony, but knowing when they're going to do this is one of life's great mysteries. They are amazing as a cut flower, but if you are relying on them for a specific event, don't count on them to do what you want them to do.

ROSES

I'm not going to lie, roses are a large investment. I've spent so much money and time on mine over the years, but I think they're worth their weight in gold. Because I grow for volume as well as quality, I have at least five plants of each variety, but even one or two can bring a huge amount of joy. I'll leave the decision to you. My best advice is to do a little research into which rose is best for your soil and the position of your growing area. You can go for bare roots, which come without foliage or flowers and arrive in a bag without soil, or potted plants (usually called 'container-grown roses'), which come with leaves and sometimes even blooms or buds, and arrive in a container with soil. I buy bare-root roses rather than potted ones because I find they tend to establish themselves faster, are less expensive and come in a wider choice

Above: peony.
Below:
disbudding.

of varieties. I plant up my bare-root roses in the winter, as soon as they arrive from the supplier, so that when the time comes for them to start growing, they're settled in and ready to go.

Best practice when caring for roses involves lots of observation. You really need to get to know your plants. An established plant needs feeding and pruning, both of which are usually done just before spring comes and they start to grow new shoots in earnest. Cut them back to around 60 cm (2 ft), and mulch the bed or container they are in. Mulching involves putting fertiliser or enriched compost on the soil as a covering to keep the soil moist, keep out weeds and feed the plant. I use horse manure, but it can be done with your own compost or bagged compost from the garden centre; just make sure it's peat-free. I also use rose feed, which isn't vital but is another step in having really healthy roses to cut from.

DISBUDDING ROSES AND DAHLIAS

While this is not essential, I find it useful for creating those really stand-out blooms for your arrangements, and it can make life easier in the future. It also gets you used to cutting the flowers. I am certainly guilty of this: not wanting to cut my flowers because they look so beautiful in the garden. It's not how we're taught to act in traditional gardens, and it can jar a little when you first take the snips to your gorgeous blooms.

Disbudding is the process of encouraging one strong, long-stemmed flower by taking out the side shoots before they really get going. This way, all the energy and nutrients are channelled into one super bud that will turn into a glorious, strong, long-stemmed flower, rather than being spread over three blooms. It feels incredibly brutal at first, but it works.

A YEAR
in the garden

My working year generally runs from autumn to autumn in terms of planning, and my harvesting season starts in spring and runs through to autumn. So, come autumn, with big events out of the way, I get down to maintenance, installing any new equipment or structures, buying and sorting seeds, and cracking on with sowing and planning what I will need for the next year.

This section details a year in the life of my garden. Use it as inspiration and a guide to the sort of jobs you can expect to do over the next twelve months, and beyond. I have become so much more in tune with the seasons through flower growing. I feel it in my body when the seasons are changing, so don't rush the process. Enjoy it – it really is magical.

Breaking down jobs month by month can make them much more manageable; you can even do it week by week if there are lots of jobs to do and you have a busy schedule with work and life in general. Life can get busy, but working on your flowers little and often and making sure to dedicate time to them regularly will make sure you get a great crop.

EARLY AUTUMN

- Decide on next year's seeds, bulbs and tubers.

- Sow hardy annuals (direct and indoors). Some great things to start now are *Ammi*, *Calendula*, *Nigella*, larkspur, *Orlaya* and *Malope* (mallow).

- Clear beds, especially if any plants have been damaged by frost.

- Cover any remaining dahlias with a portable polythene tent to protect them from frost if you need the flowers to last longer.

LATE AUTUMN/EARLY WINTER

- Cut anything you have left for drying, such as seed heads, hydrangea flower heads, *Ammi*, *Alchemilla*, grasses – anything you want to dry for arrangements over the winter.

- Continue to clear the beds.

- Begin larger projects (weather permitting), such as building a compost heap, setting up polytunnels or clearing new ground.

- Continue sowing hardy annuals. Doing this in small batches a few weeks apart (called successional sowing) helps to plug any gaps in produce when the flowers get going. It also reduces the risk of having nothing if you do unfortunately lose a batch.

- Plant any new tulip bulbs. Lift dahlias and store them in dry cardboard boxes or wooden crates. You can add sawdust, straw or newspaper to really make sure they stay dry. If they get moist, there is a real risk of them rotting.

WINTER

- Cut evergreen foliage for making wreaths (see my tips on getting hold of foliage on page 130).

- Sort through and store any dried flowers or seed heads. Hang them upside down in a cool, dry place (see page 116).

- Continue with any building or maintenance jobs.

- Days of poor weather are perfect for staying inside, keeping warm and planning the year ahead.

- Pot on any autumn-sown annuals, being sure to keep them warm and watered.

- Start activating anemone and ranunculus corms – these will be ready to go out in large pots under cover by early spring (see page 54).

- Now is a great time to cut back the leaves of hellebores to give space to new shoots and allow the flowers to shine.

LATE WINTER

- This is a great time for some rose care. For really healthy and abundant roses, chop each plant back to about 60 cm (2 ft) in height, mulch with manure or fertiliser, treat any disease and use a rose feed.

- Dig any new beds, and dig over and mulch or fertilise existing ones that you plan to use for annuals. Now is also a good time to cover beds with a weed-suppressing membrane or with cardboard (weighed down with stones or bricks); this will keep weeds at bay until you are ready to plant your first seedlings.

EARLY SPRING

- Sow hardy annuals. This can be a continuation of the ones you started to sow in autumn, but starting sowing now is also fine. Remember to look at the instructions on the seed packet so that you know when is the best time of year to sow them.

- Plant dahlias in large pots, and keep them in the greenhouse or under cover until they begin to sprout (see page 54).

- Build or install bamboo, hazel or metal structures for sweet peas and other climbing annuals to grow on, ready for the seedlings to be planted out.

- Harden off all annual seedlings and plant them out between now and mid spring (see page 41).

LATE SPRING

- Continue with digging, planting and mulching.

- Plant out dahlias.

- Continue to plant out your seedlings. As they get bigger, they will need supporting using one of the methods described on page 42.

- Feed roses again with fertiliser or specialised rose food.

- Direct sow (see page 36) any annuals that you haven't had a chance to sow yet. If you don't have a lot of indoor space, this is a great method for smaller pots and planters outside. Make sure to do it after the last frost has passed.

SUMMER

- Sow biennial seed now for earlier blooms the year after next.

- Harvest flowers for arranging.

- Tasks now revolve around deadheading and cutting back things you want to keep flowering (not letting them go to seed), and weeding.

- Keep everything well watered, especially if there is no rain for a few days. Don't neglect your perennials – they need lots of water too.

LATE SUMMER/EARLY AUTUMN

- Keep an eye on the weather forecast for frost warnings.

- Begin direct sowing and greenhouse sowing some autumn sown annuals.

- Enjoy some time with bulb and seed catalogues, picking things to grow next year.

This is a rough guide, which you will need to adapt depending on how your garden fares each season. It is also greatly dependent on the weather, of course. You might put aside a whole day for digging and then it tips down with rain! Sometimes you can be so far behind with your planting schedule that you think your year is destined to fail, but trust me, it will be OK. I've stood in my greenhouse with a cup of tea and a book waiting for the rain/hail/snow to pass enough times to know that where there's a will, there's a way.

Chapter 3:

CREATING WITH

BLOOMS

USING YOUR
flowers

You've put in the hard work, so now it's time to enjoy the spoils of your labour. There is something very magical about arranging the flowers that you have grown. You've worked hard with your blooms to get to this point, you've watched over them from tiny seeds to beautiful flowers, you've picked them gently, given them a drink, and now you can enjoy the slowness of playing with them.

My top tips for flower arranging are to take your time, enjoy the process and leave any ideas of 'perfect' at the door. In practical terms, use sharp snips and work in a cool room, if possible, to avoid stressing the cut flowers. Finally, get creative – this is your chance to express yourself in flowers!

THE BASICS

I find it really overwhelming when I open a recipe book and see what looks like a million ingredients for one dish. With that in mind, I have made sure this whole section remains as accessible as the growing side of the book. Obviously, there are things you need for flower arranging, but here I offer some of my top tips for found or recycled objects that

will serve you well, in place of spending lots of money on the 'right equipment'.

Equipment

- *String or twine*
- *Florist's or craft wire on a reel (around 24 gauge)*
- *Snips or scissors*
- *Secateurs*
- *Sticky tape or paper tape*
- *Florist's pot tape*
- *Paper (I'm one of those people who keep all their giftwrap for this very reason – there's something extremely satisfying about recycling pretty papers)*
- *Ribbon (I like to use natural, hand-dyed silks and velvets for my styling; see the Resources section on page 142 for my favourite ribbon suppliers)*
- *Card*
- *Hessian (burlap)*
- *Chicken wire*

Vessels

If you use your imagination, you will find interesting vessels wherever you look. Basically, if it's watertight you can probably put flowers in it. Not watertight? Try finding something that is and that will fit inside!

Here are some ideas for vessels:

- *Glass or ceramic vases*
- *Bowls*
- *Herb and spice jars*
- *Sauce jars (labels removed)*
- *Food cans (labels removed)*
- *Glass beer or spirits bottles (some of the fancier varieties are lovely)*

STYLING TIPS

After putting in so much effort to growing your cut flowers, you want to show them off to their best advantage and this is where styling comes in. Styling combines many different elements including composition, colour and, texture and can really allow you to express yourself. It's a very personal thing and everyone will approach it with their own tastes, which makes it quite magical. There are a few useful principles I like to use to help me when styling cut flowers:

Eco arranging

Let's talk about floral foam.
It's carcinogenic, it's not
biodegradable and, basically,
it's an environmental no-no.
I never use it in my arrangements
and, along with many in the
floristry and cut-flower-growing
community, have developed new
and better techniques for flower
arranging that concentrate on
sustainability. Other swaps I have
made are: not using single-use
plastic, such as cellophane, and
reusing plastic trays rather than
buying new ones; changing to
paper tape for my packaging;
and reusing glass jars as
delivery containers.

▸ Odd numbers draw the eye more
than the symmetry of even numbers,
so I tend to use odd numbers of vessels,
blooms and stems in my arrangements.

▸ Taking time to clean and prepare
the area where your project will go
makes all the difference to the styling,
so make sure you set the scene for
your beautiful arrangement.

▸ The personal touch always makes it.
Your own decorative paper to wrap
a bouquet, a vase you bought from
your favourite small business, a special
tablecloth from your grandma –
little things like this will make your
arrangement extra-special.

▸ Negative space is just as important
as filled space, so make sure you
consider it in your arrangements.

▸ Height is also very important when
arranging flowers – both in relation to
your vessels and in relation to the space
you are dressing. For example, a small
bookcase or shelf will need shorter stems,
a more squat vessel and maybe a more
compact arrangement, whereas a dining
table in a big room can take a taller vase,
longer stems and a wilder, more exuberant
arrangement. If you are creating a
composite arrangement of different
vessels and containers, make sure you
have a mix of tall, short and medium
stems and vessels for balance.

ADJACENT
COLOURS

BLEND
TOGETHER TO
CREATE SUBTLE
ARRANGEMENTS

COLOURS

Whichever colours make you happy are the right colours to use. Having worked for weddings, with every colour palette and combination imaginable, I've found that it's easy to get drawn into really specific ways of using colour. I've now liberated myself from that hang-up when I arrange my flowers, and I hope to help you do the same! This is not to say that we shouldn't learn how to use colour best, but we should use that knowledge as inspiration and take it in our own direction from there.

Colours that are opposite each other on the colour wheel offset each other well and make bold, contrasting displays. Colours that are next to each other will blend together and create more subtle arrangements. By all means select a colour palette, but the most important thing is to get creative and go with what you feel works best. I find that what's blooming in the garden usually goes nicely together anyway, and if we're going for a wild, abundant country style, we needn't worry too much about being strict with colour palettes. One look at a hedgerow or meadow in high summer will make it clear how, in nature, anything goes!

**THE BASIC
COLOUR WHEEL
LOOKS LIKE THIS:**

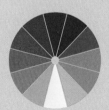

**OPPOSITE
COLOURS**

CREATE BOLD
CONTRASTING
DISPLAYS

SPRING

To me, spring feels like hope. There is potential in every bud, every blossom, every seed sown. In the garden, decisions are being made that shape the rest of the year, and ideas both big and small are taking hold, making this a time of excitement.

Pickings might be slim at this time of year, but you can make beautiful things with just a few flowers. My favourite spring-flowering blooms are tulips, daffodils, hellebores, violets, forget-me-nots (*Myosotis*), cherry and apple blossom, ranunculus and anemones.

LIVING
wreath

This lovely early spring project will provide you
with floral prettiness before your cut flowers get going.
The base is reusable, so you'll be able to rework
it all year round and still come back for another
go at this project each spring.

WHAT YOU NEED:

- *Bendy twigs (young birch and holly are best) or climbers (wisteria and clematis work well) to make the base, or a pre-made willow base (available online)*

- *Jute twine*

- *Small early spring bulb plants (Muscari, miniature daffodils)*

- *Small spring perennial plants (primroses, violets, pansies)*

- *Hessian (burlap)*

- *Foliage such as Hebe, spruces and pussy willow*

- *Snips*

WHAT TO DO:

If you are making your own base, that is where you need to start. Making sure you have good space in which to work, group a few of the thicker ends of your twigs and tie them together with the twine. Continue to add new twigs, working your way round towards the thinner ends of the twigs, tying them in as you go and forming a circle. Bend and twist the twigs around each other, if possible. Making a base can be tricky and fiddly, but I think it's worth the effort.

Now prepare your bulbs and perennials. Remove them from where they are planted, a small root clump or single bulb at a time, making sure there is still a little soil around the root or bulb. Then wrap them in small scraps of hessian to keep the soil in, like making small, soft parcels for the roots. Tie them up with twine and set to one side.

Cut each piece of foliage into 10–15 cm (4–6 in) sections. Group these in little bunches, mixing the varieties, and tie them with twine.

Now you're ready to start constructing your wreath. First, tie one end of the twine to the wreath. You will be using the twine continuously all the way round the wreath, so make sure you have plenty.

Work in one direction, with your stems or plants pointing the same way all the way around. Add a bunch of stems or a hessian parcel at a slight angle on the wreath base and wrap it tightly with twine.

Then add another bunch of stems or hessian parcel at an angle to cover up the twine and stems of the previous one (see image). Tie this one in and then move on to the next. Repeat the process, overlapping the bundles as you go and always building in the same direction.

Cover as much or as little of your wreath base as you like. It can look lovely to do just one or two thirds and leave the rest of the base bare.

Get creative and mix up your plants and foliage for a lovely springtime look.

Finally, add a loop of twine to the top so that you can hang the wreath.

CARING FOR YOUR WREATH

Once the finished wreath is hanging up, make sure to water the bulbs and plants every few days. Giving them a spritz from a spray bottle should do it, and is easily done while the wreath is hanging. However, I would not recommend hanging your wreath indoors, as moisture from the plants can damage walls and other interior fittings and water may drip on to the floor.

GATHERING
tablescape

Spring is the perfect time to gather with friends and family and celebrate the skies getting brighter, the days getting warmer and the new life bursting into action all around. A simple table arrangement is fantastic for bringing the first flowers of the year indoors to enjoy.

WHAT YOU NEED:

▶ *Five or seven bottles, jars or jugs of different heights and sizes, filled with fresh, clean water*

▶ *About three to five stems for each container, prepared and well conditioned (see page 46). We're going for pretty and delicate, so no need to worry about having anything huge – you could even do this with just one variety of flower*

▶ *Snips*

WHAT TO DO:

Place the vessels on the table where you want the arrangement to sit. (It is completely possible to do the arrangement elsewhere and place the vessels later, but I like to work in situ whenever possible.) Put taller ones towards the back or middle, with a few medium-sized ones in between and then the smallest to break things up towards the edges. Try to make them look random, as though they were just placed there without too much thought – which is usually my aim with styling.

Arrange three to five stems in each vessel. Focus on height with these, too. I would pick a single-headed flower and have that as the focal flower in a vessel, cutting it to sit fairly tall, but not so much that it looks as though it's going to take off. Then use other stems to create interest at a medium and then low height within the arrangement. You may also want to use greenery or something frothy, such as *Ammi* or *Alchemilla*, for texture.

I like to take some petals off a few flowers and sprinkle them between the vessels, giving the arrangement a 'blustery spring day' look.

TIP:
Forget-me-nots and violets are safe to eat.

As a perfect extra for your spring feast. They make really cute additions to drinks, salads and desserts.

Just make sure they're washed and that you haven't used any pesticides or chemicals on the plant in question.

CHAPTER 3: CREATING WITH BLOOMS

SIMPLE TULIP *arrangement*

The simplicity of a bunch of tulips and twigs is perfect for springtime. The clean lines of a straight-sided vase will also play nicely against the bending of the twigs and the twists and turns of the tulips.

WHAT YOU NEED:

- ▸ *Straight-sided vase or other container*

- ▸ *Twigs*

- ▸ *Tulips with lower leaves stripped from the stems (the tighter in bud they are when they are cut, the longer they will last in the arrangement; I'm using 50 stems but this project will work with a minimum of 20)*

- ▸ *Hellebores*

- ▸ *Snips*

WHAT TO DO:

Fill the vase about a third of the way up with clean water.

First, add the twigs. You want to use them to create a base structure to support the flower stems. Try to create angles so that the stems cross in the water, using the full area of the bottom of the vase to contain the stems, criss-crossing them to make a pyramid shape. Cut them to length depending on how tall your vessel is, the space you're going to be putting the arrangement in and how wild you want it to look.

Then add the tulip and hellebore stems one at a time, incorporating them into the pyramid structure around the edge and working your way in, turning the vase as you go to ensure they're evenly placed.

You will want to cut some of the stems down, as incorporating different heights will stop the arrangement looking too neat and tidy. As you build up the stems you will be creating more and more crossing stems, which should hold the arrangement in place.

Tulips have a tendency to bend and curl, you can cut them down to make their stems shorter and less likely to droop. You can use the twigs to support them, but be mindful that once the arrangement is finished the stems will reach towards the sun anyway, so we're not aiming for perfection.

Add some extra twigs at the end if you want a more dramatic arrangement.

Refresh the water every day or two by carefully tipping the water out from one side, holding the arrangement in place with your hand and topping up with clean water. Turn the vase a little at the same time to combat the tulips 'reaching' for the sun.

SUMMER

Summer is abundant. It represents fullness, growth and colour, and now you've done all the hard work over the last few months, you can enjoy the fruits of your labour. My favourite thing about summer is the last light of a long, hot day, when the sun has cooled and you can wander peacefully through the garden, harvesting, deadheading or simply sipping a cool drink.

The colours of summer are many. You can have bright and punchy or muted and soft – they're all there to choose from. I particularly like to think of dusk in the garden, cooler moments and gentle colours in the westering sun.

Even if you are only growing a few things for yourself, summer is when everything should come into its own and give you flowers to enjoy for weeks. My favourite flowers in summer are *Ammi*, scabious, *Nigella*, roses, foxgloves, sweet peas, phlox, cosmos, mint and dahlias.

WRAPPED
gift flowers

What better way to celebrate your growing efforts than
by giving a beautifully wrapped bouquet to a loved one?
If I go round to a friend's for dinner, especially in the summer
months, I feel it would be pure rudeness not to turn up with
a bunch of home-grown loveliness for my host. Taking time
to grow, cut and create a beautiful bouquet for friends and
family is a wonderful way to show love, care and creativity.

WHAT YOU NEED:

- ▸ *String*

- ▸ *About 30–40 stems, prepared and well conditioned (see page 46). Use a mix of foliage, delicate flowers and more blowsy blooms. This will work with a smaller number of flowers or even just lots of one variety*

- ▸ *Snips*

- ▸ *Paper (I've used brown paper, but you can use plain white lining paper or pretty wrapping paper)*

- ▸ *Tape (I use brown paper tape)*

- ▸ *Ribbon and gift card (optional)*

WHAT TO DO:

For the bunch of flowers:

Cut two long pieces of string (approximately 1 m/3 ft). Take one piece and make a slip knot in one end to make tying off easier. Set to one side.

I like to begin arranging by separating my flower varieties into little groups and laying them out so that I can see them all. This way nothing gets missed and you can see what colours and shapes you have to work with.

Use one hand to hold your flowers and one hand to select what you're using while you create the arrangement. I use my non-dominant hand to hold the flowers and my dominant hand to select the stems. Think of your flower-holding hand almost as a vase.

Hold your 'vase' hand open, take a stem at a time in the other hand and place them into your open palm. As you add to the bunch, cross the stems over each other, and as your hand starts to fill up, keep a good hold of them.

Think of the 'V' between your thumb and forefinger as the neck of the vase, and make sure there are no leaves below this line. The tops of your flowers should all be a similar height. I'm not into neat uniformity, but you still want to give it a nice all-round shape, and this is certainly best practice for a beginner's bunch.

If you are working with a single variety, just keep going, crossing stems, until you've used them all up. If you're going for a mixed bunch, it's best to select one stem from each pile and work your way through until you have no flowers left. If you have only a few stems of something special, such as roses, you can always poke these in from the top at the end before tying the bunch. Keeping a firm but gentle grip on the bunch, feed the stems in from the top, spacing them out and choosing where best to put them visually. Push them into place so that they are the same height as the other flowers.

Next, tie your bouquet. Take your length of string and fasten the slip knot by pulling the loose end through the loop around the stems just above where your hand is holding the bunch. The knot allows you to create a really tight tie with one hand, rather than risking letting go of the bunch.

Now we need to neaten the stem ends. You would do well not to cut them too short, since once you have gifted them or put them in your own home, the stems will benefit from being cut again, maybe even more than once, every few days, to maximise their vase life. I like to hold just below the string and measure two hands' worth of stem before holding them tightly in my fist and cutting straight across all the stems, making them all the same length.

For the paper wrapping:

Cut two rectangles from the paper. For a small bunch these should be about 30 by 60 cm (12 by 24 in); for a medium bunch about 60 by 70 cm (24 by 28 in) and for a larger bunch about 60 by 80 cm (24 by 32 in).

Fold each piece of paper in half, but at an angle. You want the points of the bottom right corner and top left corner to overlap at the top (see image), creating two points and a flat bottom. It should look a bit like a cut-out of two mountains.

With one piece of paper on top of the other, place the flowers in the middle of the 'mountains', making sure the place where you have tied the stems sits at the bottom edge of the paper.

With the flowers in the middle anchoring the paper, pull up each bottom corner of the top sheet of paper to a point and flatten a little over the flowers. You should end up with a cone shape with the stems at the point of the cone in the centre.

Secure the paper with tape, then, holding tightly on to the stems and the paper, flip the whole thing over. The tape should now be facing downwards in the middle of the second piece of paper. Repeat the step, pulling the corners up and securing with tape, as you did with the first piece of paper. Make sure you hold tightly on to the paper and stems, since these are still loose and only your hand is keeping them in place.

Now you need to tie up the whole thing. Take your second length of string and, while holding the stems and paper, wrap it around them above your hand, so that you catch the paper in securely while you tie. It doesn't matter if you squash some of the paper flat to the stems – that's meant to happen.

If you want to use a ribbon, tie it over the top of the string and style it as you like, with or without a bow. You can add a gift card to the string or ribbon, or tape one to the paper either on the inside or the outside. The stems must go in water until delivery, so don't attach any card to the stems until they're off to their final destination.

Once you've gifted them, they simply need to have the paper removed and the stems snipped slightly at an angle, and then they can be popped into a vessel of fresh, clean water. The string holding the flowers together can be cut at this point as well. Because you crossed the stems of the flowers when putting them together, they should hold their arrangement nicely.

ASYMMETRICAL
bowl arrangement

The perfect celebration of the abundance of long
summer days is a gorgeous, tumbling arrangement
using the best bits from the garden. Bring your cutting
garden inside with this wild and whimsical project,
perfect for a cool surface in the house while it's hot outside.

WHAT YOU NEED:

▸ *Chicken wire (just enough to fill your bowl when scrunched up into a loose ball)*

▸ *Gardening gloves (optional – for handling the wire)*

▸ *Bowl (I have used a cereal bowl – it doesn't have to be anything fancy, as long as it is fairly deep)*

▸ *Florist's pot tape*

▸ *About 30–50 stems, a mix of foliage, delicate flowers and more blowsy blooms, prepared and well conditioned (see page 46)*

▸ *Snips*

WHAT TO DO:

First, create the base you will be arranging into. Being careful of any sharp edges, fold and bend the chicken wire into a scrunched-up ball, as though you were loosely balling up a piece of paper. This needs to fit into the bowl. You want to end up with a mesh to anchor your stems, but make sure it's not so tight that they can't go in.

When it's ready and placed in the bowl, secure it with the pot tape. Take two strips a little longer than the top diameter of the bowl and attach them over the rim, from side to side, making a cross over the top of the bowl to hold the wire in place. Then place small strips of tape (about 10 cm/4 in long) horizontally over the ends of the tape on the outside of the bowl, to secure the structure. The tape will be taking some strain and weight, so it's important to make sure it's properly in place before beginning with the flowers. (The tape will be covered up later.)

Fill the bowl with water to a couple of centimetres (an inch or less) below the rim.

You'll be creating an asymmetrical shape with this arrangement, so mark that out first. Start by using the foliage and assessing the natural twists and turns of the stems, so that you can use these organic shapes to build your design. The lovely curve of a piece of foliage can make a great low swoop in an arrangement, and a twisty stem the perfect high point.

Start with the two outermost points, framing how wide the arrangement will be and work inwards, pushing and poking the stems into the chicken wire to secure them. The anchoring effect of the chicken wire allows you to make a much more creative shape with your arrangement than you can with just a vase, and this is key to creating an asymmetrical look.

Continue adding greenery, depending on how foliage-heavy you want the arrangement to be. Be mindful not to put too much in early on; the nature of the arrangement requires you to create some negative space in the middle.

Start filling in the gaps with more frothy, delicate flowers, bulking out the greenery

CHAPTER 3: CREATING WITH BLOOMS

framework you have created and making
sure to retain that negative space. It can
be very tempting to ram everything you
have into the bowl at this point, but we
want a relaxed, garden feel, so go slowly.

Once you're happy with the overall shape,
it's time to add your statement flowers.
Again, I am a big advocate of variety and
simplicity, so you don't have to stuff the
arrangement full of big flower heads.
Use these blooms to enhance the shape
you have already created, placing them
thoughtfully and carefully.

Next, add any last bits to create extra
texture and interest: things like grasses
and seed heads, and, for me, anything
I would describe as 'pompoms', such as
scabious or cornflower. These can provide
pops of colour and enhance the shape
you've created.

Lastly, hide the mechanics (the tape).
Your arranging may already have covered
some of it up, but get your eyes down level
with the rim of the bowl and cover any tape
you can see with foliage. Go all the way
around and make sure it is all covered.

TIP:
*Add a few large
statement flower
heads to enhance
the shape.*

GRASSES
AND SEED HEADS
CAN BE USED TO
PROVIDE TEXTURE

EASY-GROW, SINGLE-VARIETY *flower bunches*

This is a great project if you have limited growing space,
or are just starting out with annuals and have chosen to focus
on one or two varieties. It gives you the same sense of achievement
as the Wrapped Gift Flowers on page 93, but it's much cuter.
Not everyone has vast amounts of space to grow lots of different
varieties, and it really is just as nice to grow a whole pot of something
gorgeous, like sweet peas! This project is great for all the
easy-to-grow seeds mentioned on page 28.

WHAT YOU NEED:

▸ *String*

▸ *Stems of your choice, cut to a similar length, prepared and well conditioned (see page 46). If you are using a branching variety, such as scabious, and have a few offshoots on one stem, separate these off*

▸ *Paper (I've used brown paper, but you can use plain white lining paper or pretty wrapping paper)*

▸ *Tape (I use brown paper tape)*

▸ *Ribbon and gift card (optional)*

▸ *Snips*

WHAT TO DO:

For the bunch of flowers:

Start by cutting a long piece of string (approximately 1 m/3 ft) and making a slip knot in one end. Lay it out on a flat surface, from left to right in front of you.

Lay the flower stems on top of the string, with their heads at a similar height, but not neatly.

Starting from the two outside stems, gently gather the blooms together at, roughly, the halfway point of the stems.

Lift the length of string and fasten the slip knot by pulling the end through the loop around the stems near the middle where you gathered them. Don't tie them too tightly.

Now neaten the ends. You would do well not to cut them too short, since once you have gifted them or put them in your own home, they will benefit from being cut again, maybe even every few days, to maximise their vase life. I like to grasp the bunch just below the string and measure two hands' worth of stem before holding them tightly in my fist and cutting straight across all the stems, making them all the same length.

For the paper wrapping:

Cut a rectangle of paper, about 30 by 60 cm (12 by 24 in). Also, cut a length of string for securing the paper (1 m/3 ft to be safe).

Fold the piece of paper in half, but at an angle. You want the points of the bottom right corner and top left corner to overlap at the top (see image), creating two points and a flat bottom. It should look a bit like a cut-out of two mountains.

Place the flowers in the middle of the 'mountains', making sure the place where you have tied the stems sits at the bottom edge of the paper.

With the flowers in the middle anchoring the paper, pull up one of the bottom corners of the paper to the opposite corner and then tuck around the flowers as you begin to roll the flowers up into a cone. Secure the paper with tape.

Nip in the paper near the bottom of the cone and secure it with the other piece of string.

If you want to use a ribbon, tie it over the top of the string and style it as you like, with or without a bow. You can add a gift card to the string or ribbon, or tape one to the paper on the inside or outside. The stems must go in water until delivery, so don't attach any card to the stems until they're off to their final destination.

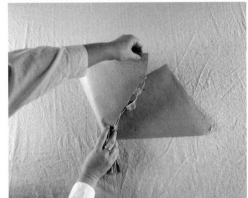

Once you've gifted them, they simply need to have the paper and string removed and the stems snipped slightly at an angle, and then they can be popped into an appropriately sized vessel of fresh, clean water.

AUTUMN

To say I love all seasons equally would be a small lie.
I have cherished and favourite moments during all of them, but there
is a very special place in my heart for autumn: the rich, beautiful
colours of the changing leaves, hunting out the best coats, scarves
and boots from the cupboard, and the slanting, golden light
as the days shorten. The fact that my birthday sits perfectly in the
middle of it all helps to give autumn its special status for me.

Autumn is all about golds, yellows, oranges, reds and browns,
as though the summer sun is leaving its mark on the landscape before
handing things over to winter. Things are usually winding down
in the garden by this time, but there is still plenty to enjoy.
The best bits of the season, for me, are dahlias, chrysanthemums,
beech leaves, fruiting branches of apple and blackberry, ferns,
scabious, *Calendula* and all the various seed heads.

ABUNDANT VASE
arrangement

This is the perfect project for celebrating the last
floral delights of the summer. By bringing the mellow
autumnal mood inside, as the temperature drops,
and creating a beautiful indoor display, you can stretch
out the enjoyment of your flowers for a little longer.

WHAT YOU NEED:

► *Around 30–50 stems, prepared and well conditioned (see page 46). I have used a mix of foliage, delicate flowers and heavier-headed blooms. If all you have is smaller, more delicate flowers, you may need more.*

► *Glass or ceramic vase filled with water*

► *Snips*

WHAT TO DO:

Starting with foliage, put at least 5 stems into the vase. Try to create angles so that the stems cross in the water, using the full area of the bottom of the vase to contain the stems. The bare part of the stem should go below the water line, and the leaves come just over the top of the vase rim. This may mean cutting the stems a little shorter than when they were harvested; remember always to cut at an angle.

Next, add frothy and wispy flowers and more foliage if you have it, going around the vase, crossing the stems over to make a criss-cross base in the water. Work your way into the middle and use the angles you have made with the outer stems to anchor the middle bits.

Make sure you cut the stem of each flower as you add it. It can be easy to forget this and just add them all at the length they were harvested, but this will create an unstable base with top-heavy flowers

flopping around. It's important to work with the vessel, using its height and shape to inform the lengths of your stems and the shape of your arrangement.

Once you're happy with your criss-cross base, it's time to add any larger blooms you have. Do this strategically and in odd numbers (fives and threes usually work best). Spread them evenly throughout the arrangement. These are the statement pieces in your arrangement, but you don't want to crowd them in – a few will be enough for that 'country garden'-style display. If you don't have any big blooms, just carry on adding your lovely delicate flowers until the vase looks nice and full – it will be just as gorgeous.

Now it's time to add interest with any blooms you want to use to create shape. I usually pick a few pieces that I just really like the shape of, maybe some grasses and lovely wild-looking bits, and dot them throughout. Adding height creates that all-important negative space, and adding texture creates interesting dimensions to your arrangement.

EASY AUTUMNAL *garland*

This is the perfect time of year for gathering the last
bits from the garden and drying them out, and what
better way to use them than in a decorative garland?
Hang it inside to remind you of the wonderful things
you've grown this year and inspire you to plan for
another year in the garden – all with a cup of tea,
of course. As part of this project we will learn how
to dry flowers and seed heads to preserve them.

WHAT YOU NEED:

- *About 20–40 stems of seed heads, grasses and flowers that dry well (see box)*

- *String*

- *Ribbon (optional)*

- *Something to hang your garland on*

- *Snips*

WHAT TO DO:

Cut the stems to 15–20 cm (6–8 in) in length, making little piles of them as you go.

Selecting from the piles you made, create bundles of between 2 and 5 stems, tying them with string about 5 cm (2 in) from the bottom.

Tie these bundles to a longer piece of string, leaving a 20–30 cm (8–12 in) gap between bundles. You can also alternate the bundles with lengths of ribbon to add some decorative colour if you like.

Hang the string up so the flower and seed heads are all pointing down, and leave to dry out for a few weeks, this can be in situ where you plan to have the garland or any dry room.

Once dry, you can either leave them hanging and enjoy them as they are, or snip off individual bundles and pop them in pots and jars around the house. You can also use them in the winter projects on pages 125 and 133.

BEST FLOWERS FOR DRYING:

Seed heads, e.g.
poppy (*Papaver*), love-in-a-mist (*Nigella damascene*), *Scabiosa stellata*

Grasses, e.g.
Briza, Lagurus, Panicum elegans 'Frosted Explosion', *Pennisetum*

Flowers, e.g.
Larkspur (*Consolida ajacis*)

Bishop's flower (*Ammi majus*)

Hydrangea (*Hydrangea*)

Lavender (*Lavandula*)

Rose buds (*Rosa*)

Statice (*Limonium*)

Yarrow (*Achillea*)

Love-lies-bleeding (*Amaranthus*)

TIP:
*Drying stems tend
to shrink as they
lose moisture.*

Make sure to keep an eye
on them. If the string holding
them together feels a little slack,
tighten them up a little.

DAHLIA COMPOTE *arrangement*

I've mentioned it before, and I'll say it again, dahlias are my favourite flower ever! They make me think of early autumn days because, while the trees are changing colour, the dahlias are already putting on their show of the best hues of the season. The 'compote' element of this arrangement comes from the name of the footed bowls traditionally used for serving fruits or nuts. There's no reason why dahlias can't be part of the offering though!

WHAT YOU NEED:

- *Chicken wire (just enough to fill the bowl when scrunched up into a loose ball)*
- *Gardening gloves (optional – for handling the wire)*
- *Footed bowl*
- *Clear florist's pot tape (or another strong tape, such as duct tape, cut into strips)*
- *15–20 stems of mixed dahlias*
- *Other stems if you wish (I've used* Ammi, Calendula *and phlox)*
- *Snips*

WHAT TO DO:

First create the base you will be arranging into. Taking care with the sharp ends, crumple the chicken wire into a ball. This should fit into the bowl. You want to end up with a mesh into which you can anchor your stems, but not so tight that they can't go in.

Place the wire ball in the bowl. Take two strips of tape a little longer than the top diameter of the bowl and attach them over the rim, from side to side, making a cross over the top of the bowl to hold the wire in place. Then secure the structure with small strips of tape (about 10 cm/4 in long) horizontally over the ends of the tape on the outside of the bowl. It's important to make sure the wire and tape are properly in place

before beginning with the flowers, because they will bear weight. (We will hide the pieces of tape later.)

Fill the bowl with water to a couple of centimetres (1 in) below the rim.

Using these larger-headed blooms means we're going for a bolder style of arrangement. Frame the arrangement with a few blooms to begin with, using the tallest of your stems to dictate the top and deciding on the width on all four sides of the bowl. Place the lower-down blooms close to the tape to hide where you have attached the tape to the side of the bowl. (Be careful with the flower heads, as dahlia petals do bruise easily.)

Once you're happy with these structural points, it's now just a matter of filling in the gaps, deciding which flowers to place deeper in the arrangement and which to leave protruding. Use your creativity – what do you think looks best? It's as much about enjoying the process as it is about making something that looks 'perfect'.

If you are adding extra ingredients, pop these in last, using them sparingly just to complement the dahlias and fill in any spaces.

WINTER

For me, winter means digging out my biggest jumpers, doing lots
of planning for the next twelve months in the garden, and gathering with
my nearest and dearest in the warmth. It's also a time for reflection and
taking stock and, while I miss the garden when it's not in bloom, there are
still many wonderful things about the colder months. A crisp, cold morning,
a warming mug of something delicious and twinkling lights on short,
dark days are simple pleasures that make winter special for me.

The colours of winter are muted, but there is beauty right there in the
green and the brown. There are also pops of sandy yellow in catkins
and grasses and a punch of red in berries, so if you make an effort to look
for the subtle colours of winter you won't be disappointed.

Flowers are few and far between, but the best bits of the season are
hellebores, early daffodils, *Muscari*, catkins from trees such as alder, hazel
and silver birch, and evergreen foliage such as spruce, yew and *Cotoneaster*.

WINTER
Wreath

When the colder months set in and you're missing the haven that the garden has been through the summer, making home a welcoming, cosy and comforting environment is key. What better way to bring some special warmth into your home than with a winter wreath either welcoming you at the door or hanging cosily over the fireplace (or both)?

WHAT YOU NEED:

▸ *Twigs to make a base, or a ready-made willow base (available online)*

▸ *Foliage*

▸ *Dried seed heads and grasses*

▸ *Florist's or craft wire on a reel (around 24 gauge)*

▸ *String*

▸ *Ribbon*

▸ *Snips*

WHAT TO DO:

As with the spring wreath (see page 77), if you are making your own base, that is where you need to start. Making sure you have good space to work, group a few of the thicker ends of your twigs and tie them together with string. Continue to add new twigs, working your way round towards the thinner ends of the twigs, tying them in as you go and forming a circle. Bend and twist the twigs around each other if possible.

Next, cut the foliage and dried ingredients and sort into piles, ready to attach to the base. The length of your stems will determine how wide your wreath ends up, so think about this before you cut them all too short. If you're unsure, you could do a few to begin with, to test how you like the width when they're attached. It's a design process where you're in control, and playing with the lengths of the stems

and the size of the wreath can give really interesting results.

Now attach the wire, still on its reel, firmly to the wreath. You will be using the wire continuously all the way around the wreath.

You're now going to create little bundles with your cut pieces and attach them to the base. Gather 3–5 stems at a time and place them at an angle on the base. Wrap the wire tightly a few times around the bundle to hold them in place.

Then move on to the next bundle, placing it on top of the first one, at an opposing angle but pointing in the same direction. The aim is to cover the wire and stems of the first bundle with this second one. Now wire it in place.

Continue in this way until you have filled as much of the wreath base as you want to. It can look really effective with one third or two thirds covered, but by all means do the whole thing if you like!

Finish off by knotting the wire back on itself and tucking the ends into the wreath. Add a loop of string to the top of the wreath so that you can hang it.

If you want to add ribbon, now is the time. Add it to either top or bottom, with a bow or just simple trailing ends – the choice is yours.

TABLESCAPE
for a feast

Winter is a time for keeping warm, staying indoors
and enjoying comfort food with friends. I've always wanted
to play hostess, ever since I was little and had tea parties with
my toys, and this has followed me through to my adult life.
Eating with friends and family is one of life's true joys,
and I always want to make it look as good as it feels to gather
on a cold day in a warm house with the people you love.

The centrepiece of this display is a garland that will run
down the middle of the table. It can be as large as you have
material for, but even a delicate garland runner will look
lovely once you've styled it.

WHAT YOU NEED:

- *Evergreen foliage, berries and/or dried flowers and grasses*

- *Pinecones*

- *Florist's or craft wire on a reel (around 24 gauge)*

- *Dinner candles, candle-holders, tea lights and holders, fabric runner and wire fairy lights*

- *Snips*

WHAT TO DO:

Cut the foliage and dried ingredients down into manageable pieces. To decide how long to cut the stems, determine how large you want your garland to be. The longer the stems, the wider the garland, whereas shorter stems will result in a more compact, neat garland.

Now make up bunches, using 5 or 6 stems in each bunch. Mix different varieties together in each one. To incorporate your pinecones, twist a 15 cm (6 in) length of wire around the lower scales and add them to the bunch.

Tie the end of the wire to the stems of the first bunch to bind them tightly.

Lay the second bunch on top of the first, pointing in the same direction and covering the stems of the first. Take the wire and bind the stems of the second bunch to the stems of the first. You should now have two bunches tied together.

Repeat this with the next bunch and the next, building up the layers and extending the garland. Carry on until you have just one bunch left, which will face the opposite direction to the rest of the garland. Place it over the stems of the penultimate bunch and attach it using the wire. Tie off the wire and tuck the ends into the garland. You can happily finish the project here and lay it on your dinner table as a centrepiece. However, for a special gathering I like to add some twinkling fairy lights and candles.

A NOTE ON EVERGREEN FOLIAGE

Here are a few tips to help you get your hands on some:

- Ask friends and family if you can use what's in their garden.

- Ask your local florist or flower farmer if they would be willing to get some for you.

- If you are foraging for personal use you must always have permission from the land owner. Please familiarise yourself with local laws. There is more information about foraging on page 142.

DRIED MEADOW *arrangement*

This is a fantastic project to use up any dried
bits you have left from making your autumn
arrangements. It will look lovely on a mantelpiece
or windowsill and, because dried material makes
great shadows on the walls when the low winter
sun is shining, you'll have something pretty
to look at to remind yourself of the garden.

WHAT YOU NEED:

- ▸ *Chicken wire (cut to a similar size to the tray you are using)*

- ▸ *Gardening gloves (optional – for handling the wire)*

- ▸ *Long, thin tray or plate (mine is 35 cm/14 in long)*

- ▸ *Clear florist's pot tape*

- ▸ *Dried stems (I used about 70–80 stems, but you can do this project with a smaller number)*

- ▸ *Snips*

WHAT TO DO:

First, make the base for your arrangement. Scrunch up the chicken wire into a sausage shape that will fit on to the tray you are using, wearing gardening gloves if necessary to protect your hands. You want to end up with a mesh to anchor your stems, but make sure it's not so tight that they can't go in.

Tape over the wire sausage in a few different places to stick it to the bottom of the tray. I would also secure the ends of the tape with a little extra tape to really stick it down.

Now add the dried ingredients. I like to use one variety at a time, starting with something bushy or frothy such as *Alchemilla*, which is also great for covering your tape at the bottom. Poke the stems into the chicken wire along the length of the tray, spacing them out evenly. By using

one variety at a time you ensure that you spread what you have of that ingredient evenly throughout the arrangement.

Carry on until the chicken wire is covered with all your ingredients, making sure to cover up the tape you've used to secure the arrangement to the tray. If you don't have enough dried material to make it look bulky, don't worry – it's meant to be airy and light, like the hedgerows and meadows in the winter, and sometimes sparsity is just as beautiful.

Index

Resources

EQUIPMENT AND STYLING

For beautiful props and planters:
Harry and Frank
www.harryandfrank.co.uk

Natural dyed ribbons and fabric:
Laik Style
www.laikstyle.co.uk

Planters and general garden equipment:
Garden Trading
www.gardentrading.co.uk

SEEDS AND PLANTS

United Kingdom
Sarah Raven
www.sarahraven.com

Suttons
www.suttons.co.uk

Chiltern Seeds
www.chilternseeds.co.uk

Eagle Sweet Peas
www.eaglesweetpeas.co.uk

Green and Gorgeous
www.greenandgorgeousflowers.
co.uk/seeds

Fryer's Roses
www.fryersroses.co.uk

David Austin Roses
www.davidaustinroses.co.uk

Peter Nyssen
www.peternyssen.com

United States
Territorial Seed Company
www.territorialseed.com

Botanical Interests
www.botanicalinterests.com

Ardelia Farm
www.ardeliafarm.com

Baker Creek Heirloom Seeds
www.rareseeds.com

International
Plant World Seeds
www.plant-world-seeds.com/

Advice on Foraging
www.woodlandtrust.org.uk/
visiting-woods/things-to-do/
foraging/foraging-guidelines/

www.forageculture.com/
foraging-laws

WHERE TO BUY CUT FLOWERS IF YOU WANT TO SUPPLEMENT YOUR OWN

United Kingdom
Flowers from the Farm
www.flowersfromthefarm.co.uk

United States
Philippa Craddock
(for a great list of flower farms)
www.philippacraddock.com/
flower-farms-united-states-of-
america

International
Philippa Craddock
(for international flower farms)
www.philippacraddock.com/
flower-farms

Buy local and shop small
wherever possible.

WORKSHOPS

If you'd like to learn more
about growing and arranging
flowers, I host workshops at
my studio in Derbyshire in
the UK. You can find out more
and how to book on my website:
www.francesandrose.co.uk.

There will also be fantastic
workshops and flower schools
in your local area, so make sure
to look up flower growers and
florists near you to see what
they have on offer.

Acknowledgements

Mum, I would know none of this without you. Thank you for all the support, time, patience and tea. You will never know how grateful I am for everything you have done for me, both in my business and in life. I owe all my creativity to you, and I am so glad you and Dad never wanted me to have a 'sensible' job, but always just wanted me to be happy.

To Alan, for always being there: the good, the bad, the tantrums, the croissants. You have supported me through the highs and lows of running Frances and Rose. You are on our team no matter what, and when I'm taking myself a little too seriously, you pull me back with the wonderful silliness that is living with you. Our house is full of smiles and laughter and paws (Burt).

Dad and Stephen, I'm sure sometimes you must wonder what it is that Mum and I actually do with all these flowers, but you always believe in me and tell me I'm going to be great. Thank you for everything.

Fred and Ted, welcoming me into your family means everything. Your care and support for Alan and myself are something for which I will be grateful for the rest of my life.

Susie, my unofficial life consultant, what couldn't we figure out over waffles and coffee, hey? You inspire me so much and I am lucky to know you. I am ever grateful for all your unwavering support. I am also grateful for the dresses – the beautiful, beautiful dresses!

Daisy, for the tea and the toast, and everything else!

Elle, our Tuesdays will forever be my favourite part of being self-employed. I can't believe how lucky I am to benefit from the warmth and constancy of your friendship. Thank you for everything.

Emily, thank you for being my friend forever. Thank you for all the amazing help and advice on this project and for always being so proud of me.

Char and Emma (and my little Ellie – you are the future), for all the years, all the memories, all the fun and all the support. When business gets too much I have sanctuary in your friendship.

Kath, we're in this together, until the bitter, flowery end! Your support and advice have always and will always mean the world to me. Tim isn't too bad either!

Gemma, you might think I have taught you things, but you have taught me so much as well. Thank you for letting me use your perfect space for the book and for being such a supportive friend throughout.

Meelie, for all the listening and the support.

Kerry and Lauren K., you are two of the wisest women I have ever met. Your belief and faith in my ability are so encouraging and I'll never get tired of talking everything through with you.

Gill, your passion for flower growing will always be an inspiration to me. You are so knowledgeable and organised and you grow the most beautiful flowers I've ever seen! I want to be just like you when I grow up.

Kajal, you took a chance on me and made my dreams come true. I won't ever be able to repay you for your faith in me. You're incredibly talented and your warmth and support are so energising. Chelsea, you have been a joy to work with, so supportive and encouraging. Thank you so much for all your help and hard work on shaping this project into something marvellous!

Lauren O., Lisa and Katheryn for pushing me to make this book in the first place and helping me to take the initial steps towards my goals – you don't know how much you shaped this thing.

Everyone from the amazing Flowers from the Farm, who have always inspired me and made me feel part of something bigger and more important than just growing flowers. You are the most generous people with the warmest hearts and the best cups of tea.

Finally, the biggest thank you of them all, to you, the reader. For buying this book, for coming to my workshops, for chatting with me on Instagram – you're one of the best parts of the job and I'm so happy to have you as part of my journey.

ABOUT THE AUTHOR

Marianne Slater is a floral designer and cut-flower workshop host working in Derbyshire, UK. She has always felt most comfortable getting creative with unusual materials and natural objects, and feeling freedom in her creativity.

Marianne started her journey to growing cut flowers with a simple floristry class, which soon blossomed into a wedding florals business, Frances and Rose, established in 2013. She's a firm believer in the #grownnotflown ethos and promotes its environmental message in all that she does.